"*By its simple, clear personal stories from the people connected with it directly, the North Platte Canteen comes alive and makes for interesting, informative reading for all ages.*" *- Lloyd Synovec, North Platte, Nebraska*

Penned by Charlotte Endorf
Illustrated by Ethan Nelson

BLESS YOUR HEARTS
⇛ *The North Platte Canteen* ⇛

Bringing
history
to life!
Charlotte

outskirtspress
DENVER, COLORADO

Bless Your Hearts
The North Platte Canteen
All Rights Reserved.
Copyright © 2013 Charlotte Endorf
v2.0 r1.1

Outskirts Press, Inc.
http://www.outskirtspress.com

ISBN: 978-1-4787-1730-0

Library of Congress Control Number: 2012921099

Outskirts Press and the "OP" logo are trademarks belonging to Outskirts Press, Inc.

PRINTED IN THE UNITED STATES OF AMERICA

Table of Contents

A steam engine that would bring the soldiers to the Canteen.

The railroad depot in North Platte. The Canteen sign is to the right.

A close-up picture of the front of the canteen.

The ladies delivering snacks and magazines to those that could not get off of the train.

Sending the men off with a wave.

A yippee of joy rose from the crowd as open windows in the train revealed soldiers. At last the train had arrived! Only it wasn't the right group. It was a troop train from Kansas. But the sight of their smiling faces, their friendly spirits, and their joy at seeing such a reception, as people boarded the train with gifts originally intended for the North Platte troop train, was too much for the crowd. They gathered around the men, gave the gifts they had brought for their own families, and wished them well.

When the train left, the soldiers enthusiastically waved goodbye. Thumbs were sticking up out of open windows and mothers were dabbing their eyes. Some didn't bother with handkerchiefs, they just cried and didn't care who saw them. Perhaps volunteers were murmuring, "Bless your hearts" to the troops as the train pulled away, with those inside saying exactly the same.

The volunteers (including Rae Wilson - in the front) wearing "V" for victory.

George Wilson, Rae's father, takes on janitor tasks.

In the happy group that jammed the depot, no one was more thrilled than pretty 26-year-old **Rae Wilson**, a drugstore sales girl whose brother served in the military. And Rae Wilson decided to meet all the trains going through North Platte to give other men the same send-off. The day after the troop train visit, she suggested that a canteen be opened to make the trips more entertaining for the soldiers. She offered her services without charge.

Rae took time off from her job and got busy. She called just about everyone in town, asking merchants for candy, magazines, and anything else they would give. She lined up housewives to contribute cakes and cookies, and asked younger women to be on hand at the station to dish up coffee and conversation for the soldiers.

William Jeffers, president of the Union Pacific Railroad at the time the Canteen was in operation.

Eight days later, on Christmas Day of 1941, another troop train pulled in at North Platte, filled with soldiers anticipating an uneventful holiday train ride. They too were greeted by a crowd of smiling young volunteers and a canteen. First the volunteers worked out of the Cody Hotel. Later, railroaders arranged to let them use a little shack beside the tracks, which saved lots of walking. Then Miss Wilson convinced **William M. Jeffers**, president of the Union Pacific Railroad, to turn over a large dining room in the depot to the canteen.

The movement began to grow. Soon many other communities were sharing in what became one of the greatest examples of cooperation and generosity to come out of World War II.

Anselmo and Merna Donation List

53 Birthday cakes
127 fried chickens
258 dozen cupcakes
327 dozen cookies
41 quarts of cream
73 pounds of coffee
163 dozen eggs
186 dozen doughnuts
47 pounds of sugar
41 quarts of pickles
9 pounds of ham
16 dozen buns
160 loaves of bread
40 popcorn balls
50 pounds of sandwich meat

Elberta as a young girl.

The canteen had a rule that minors without a parent had to be sixteen to enter. Lots of children helped too. **Elberta Brummert** was nine years old in 1945 when she was allowed to skip school to go along for either her Salem Lutheran Church or the entire Eustis, Nebraska community. Records indicate the small villages of Anselmo and Merna brought in one day: 53 birthday cakes, 127 fried chickens, 258 dozen cupcakes, 327 dozen cookies, 41 quarts of cream, 73 pounds of coffee, 163 dozen eggs, 186 dozen doughnuts, 47 pounds of sugar, 41 quarts of pickles, 3 $\frac{1}{2}$ crates of oranges, 9 pounds of ham, 16 dozen buns, 160 loaves of bread, a bushel of popcorn, 40 popcorn balls, 50 pounds of sandwich meat, 9 meat loaves, 1,800 pints of milk, 4 cartons of cigarettes, 4 decks of cards and $440 in cash donations. Elberta shared the back seat of her parents' 1930 black Chevrolet with food to be delivered.

According to canteen records, the total value of food donated during its operation would be a guess. Only during March 1945 was an exact list of food kept. Sent or brought in then were 40,161 homemade cookies, 30,679 hard boiled eggs, 6,939 cup, loaf, and birthday cakes, 2,845 pounds of sandwich meat, and a dozen or more other articles in like proportions! Retail value of the items at that time was about $6,250.

Elberta was in awe of the Union Pacific Railroad depot. She had never seen such a large building. The interior was huge and sounds echoed when it was empty. The food and drink were laid out on long tables.

Elberta couldn't believe the size of trains that arrived. Service personnel would get off the train and take off on a dead run for the depot. She had never seen men in uniform before. They were fascinating. The men only had a short stop of 10 minutes. She remembers **Lloyd Synovec** sitting down at the piano to play, and before long it became a party-like atmosphere.

Lloyd made the canteen piano "talk" when he sat down to it. It almost seemed to come to life! In March of 1945, Lloyd's military coach passed through North Platte. He recalls playing "Don't Sit Under The Apple Tree" and "In The Mood". A crowd gathered around the piano when Lloyd began to play. Some sang, while others danced. Although most of his time was spent entertaining, he was sent away with nourishing food and drink when he rejoined his Navy buddies aboard the train. Lloyd's home was in Pierce, Nebraska. He passed through the canteen only one time.

Lloyd playing for a crowd.

The actual piano Lloyd played is now displayed at the North Platte museum.

The railroad hired boys at the age of fifteen who were willing to work for fifty cents an hour. **John Spelts** worked as a railrunner. His job was to oil the wheels on the trains as needed. John was a very skinny kid and was surprised he was hired, but worked very hard to prove he was worth it.

His mother was in charge of the telephone office. The government paid him to run messages for them. If he had to go ten miles it cost a quarter. Otherwise, it was only ten cents. Death messages were free of charge.

Bob Runner
as a young boy.

Robert Runner was a boy interested in watching what was going on at the depot. While the trains were stopped in the station and the G.I.s were going to the canteen, Bob watched a railroad employee walk the length of the train oiling the wheels. The wheels had babbat bearings and were lubricated with a wad of cotton soaked in oil. The worker had a long hook to lift the lid on the axle and an oil can with a long spout to dispense the oil. The lid would drop closed with a loud clap.

Steam engines were often exchanged for an engine with a full load of coal and water to save time in the yards. Train crews were also changed in North Platte. Many of the passenger cars used during the war were old and in poor shape, given an extension of life to haul servicemen and women.

Ann and her mother around the time that they were making popcorn balls for the soldiers.

Ann Perlinger was only nine years old when her mom asked her to help make popcorn balls for Paxton, Nebraska's assigned day at the canteen. Ann had heard the older girls were putting their names in the balls and getting letters back in the mail. She wondered if that could possibly happen for her as well. She dared to try!

Another lady had the same name as she did in their small town. Ann's mother got a startling phone call. "Had *little Ann* written to a serviceman?" Ann's mother immediately quizzed her. Ann told her mother she had put her name in one popcorn ball. Her mom made her write back immediately and tell the serviceman she was only nine.

He wasn't angry! Instead, he was just thrilled to get mail of any type.

Gene with one of his famous auctioned shirts. Hirschfeld's donated the shirts to him for the cause.

Gene Slattery was a nine-year-old with some pesky goats. His mother was fed up and told him to get rid of the animals so he went to the sale barn with his dad to do just that. He'd heard about the canteen and how they needed money. One thing led to another. A friend egged him on, saying that he'd sell the shirt off his back and sure enough, that's what Gene started to do in the name of the North Platte canteen.

His shirt would sell over and over again. The most it sold for was $1,700! Gene started winning awards for his good deeds. He became a kid hero. A local store in North Platte, **Hirschfeld's,** gave him a constant supply of nice shirts to auction.

June Kerkman, her twin sister, and their girlfriends found it great fun, when they were in high school, to walk the short distance from the Catholic school in North Platte and volunteer their time. Their helping hands were needed to distribute tiny milk jars the servicemen used to gulp their ice-cold milk. An entire birthday cake was given to those who had a birthday, a truly exciting event for them. This tradition started in 1942. Area children gave up their own birthday cakes to the canteen. Being a "platform girl" to give directions, distribute fruit, magazines, decks of cards and sandwiches from the baskets was a touching experience. By 1945, there were 1,000 requests a day for reading matter.

As the war progressed and military hospital trains began to roll through North Platte with the war wounded, volunteers also rounded up razors, blades, canes, toothbrushes, and jigsaw puzzles for care baskets to be sent on the trains. At its peak, retail value of what was served daily was estimated at $5,000. Think of what the dollar value would be today!

Pearl

Pearl Nickerson came along with her mom and the other ladies from Farnam, Nebraska at age sixteen. She has fond memories of being a platform girl. Oh, so many deviled eggs, angel food cakes, apples, and oranges lined the long tables.

Everybody had a good time in their short ten minutes at the canteen. The majority of those serving our country were men in their late teens to early twenties. She wrote to a couple of them for awhile. One was from Ohio. All came out of the canteen smiling, ready to serve our country with pride.

A photo of John
while he was in
the service.

Most servicemen ran as fast as they could into the canteen—**John Zgud** happened to get caught on camera without his military hat. The picture eventually showed up on postcards all over the nation.

John had the best job that he, as a young man in his twenties, ever thought he'd have. He was a supervisor at a plane factory. However, he was not satisfied. John felt when the war was over he would be snubbed. Maybe he would have a nice suit and money in the bank but his friends would have served our country! So, he wanted to enlist. His employer didn't agree. Finally, after lots of arguing back and forth John left for the Army Air Corps, now the Air Force.

John flew his first mission August 30, 1944. His plane was called the "Big Time Operator". His work was with bombs. He would walk a very narrow catwalk in the back of the plane at 28,000 feet, breaking icicles off his chin in sometimes 58 below zero weather conditions. He was responsible for jiggling a screwdriver or pliers to make the bombs work correctly. Berlin was an extremely bad place to be. The planes usually ended up damaged. Everybody would sweat—just like in the movies.

His crew was listed as number one. This was exciting but also scary. The Germans tried hardest to hit the number one target. As a sort of "peace of mind" each soldier was equipped with a cloth escape map. This map was secretly tucked into their pocket like a handkerchief. If lost they could find their way back at night. John never had to use it.

Betty Matz found the canteen to be very friendly on her brief stay as she traveled to enter the Navy Waves for four years (making $21 a month) to serve our country. She enjoyed the delicious sandwiches. It was a good experience. She liked everyone she met.

The underlying feeling of everyone involved was, "Let's get this war over!"

Wayne Hoffman and a buddy from Grant, Nebraska entered the Marines. They stopped at the canteen before being shipped overseas for over three years. He claimed one word explained the canteen. That word was "wonderful"! Wayne went to artillery training while his buddy went to radio school.

Lorene on the day of Charlotte's interview.

Volunteers from over 125 communities assisted with the canteen. They came as individuals and groups from churches, schools, lodges, auxiliaries, employee clubs, etc. In those years sugar, coffee, meat, butter, and gasoline were rationed. Families had to ration themselves tighter in order to meet the canteen's needs. Groups from distant towns pooled gasoline rations to enable their communities' volunteers to make the drive to North Platte and take their turn working at the canteen.

Lorene Huebner received her driver's license before her girlfriend had one. Her dad threw her the car keys and the two would be off to the canteen for another much-needed stint of "straightening magazines". The piano was usually being played by a talented soldier "letting go of his or her emotions".

As each troop train arrived, the room became so full that people stood shoulder to shoulder. The food was good, but it was for the servicemen and women. Lorene took no time to eat. She was much too busy.

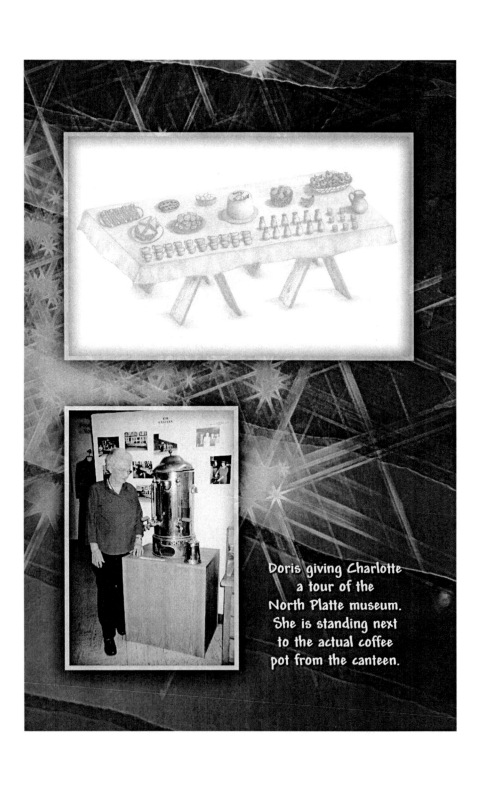

Doris giving Charlotte
a tour of the
North Platte museum.
She is standing next
to the actual coffee
pot from the canteen.

Doris Kugler was twenty-four and married. Her husband, Bill, realized that before long he would be drafted. He dreamed of being in the Navy, however, he knew the draft would put him in the Army. So, he enlisted in the Navy before he was drafted. The couple lived in Broken Bow, Nebraska.

Doris found it her patriotic duty to serve at the canteen as much as possible while her husband served our country. She made many beef, egg, and ham salad sandwiches. The sandwiches were placed directly on the table without wrapping. Nobody wore hairnets or gloves. The remarkable thing is—in a different era—nobody got sick!

Maurine Lydiatt lived in Lodgepole, Nebraska. She was also in her twenties and her husband was in the Air Corps. A group of patriotic girls crammed her car as full as they could. When it was her turn, she drove the 1937 black Chevrolet 100 miles to North Platte every two weeks. It was always a big day.

She would take ground pork and chicken for sandwiches. Sometimes it was just all mixed together. The mayonnaise was homemade. There were no potato chips. Lots of fresh fruit such as apples and oranges, along with pies, sheet cakes, and the decorated birthday cakes.

Francis Hunt lived across the tracks from the depot. He was a train watcher as a kid and loved to watch the trains and people. The train didn't wait for anybody. Those servicemen and women had ten minutes. In they went for their free meal and out they came to serve their country.

George Jensen served our Army Infantry in many aspects. He came from a family of fourteen. George did what he was told and took weapons training to do more whenever asked. He served in the Pacific. George was seriously wounded but didn't want to up-set his parents so he just told them he was nicked in the side.

He was part of the paratroops and spent time on islands and in the jungle. George saw a lot, but in all that he saw, he never was sent through North Platte to the canteen nor did he ever see a canteen to compare to it.

The girl he later married, **Darlene Jensen** fulfilled her patriotic duty in high school when her Zion Lutheran Church from Gothenburg, Nebraska and her 3-H (not 4-H) Club went to North Platte. She went with her mom.

Paul Kjar (pronounced Care) had been in the Navy since 1936. He had been out of the military for two years when he was drafted into the Army. There were about 150 men at the recruiting station. Paul realized that he could earn an extra $50 per month if he took parachute training. So, he signed up!

The way train lines were organized, troop trains stopped in North Platte. He hadn't seen his youngest sister Patricia in the years since he had been away in the military. She was there. Lots of hugging was going on. His buddies gave Paul a bad time because he made the girls cry.

When he got back on the train, it wasn't his birthday but his little sister saw to it that he and his buddies had five cakes. Enough for snacks until they got to North Carolina.

A photo of Maurice while
he was in the service.

Maurice Stalaker was stationed in North Platte for the Naval Air Corps. It was the first place he was stationed. He wore his everyday clothes as he traveled by bus from the old hospital in town to the airport for training to become a fighter pilot.

Every once in a while he and his buddies would go to the canteen to look around. It was very crowded because an average of thirty passenger trains came through each day. Maurice was sent all over the place after North Platte. He remembers going to Kansas, the east coast, Florida, California, and Oregon. He doesn't remember another canteen like North Platte. He stayed in San Diego, California for a month with orders to go to help at Pearl Harbor. He didn't make it, though, because the war was over! He had served our country for three years.

Margaret Stuart was old enough to drive in 1941. She remembers the food preparation involved when it was Cozad's turn to help. Many sandwiches were assembled. The soldiers especially enjoyed deviled eggs.

The piano played, soldiers ate, people sang—soldier after soldier was amazed by the generosity of the good people and the fact that they were required to pay absolutely nothing.

Martha Schroeder had a brother serving in the military. Her community club in Eustis was helping at the Canteen for a day. She was assigned the job of platform girl, and went aboard the train to distribute donuts and apples to the soldiers who were wounded.

She had a problem. Her husband did not want her to go. He had heard the soldiers whistled at pretty girls. She felt it was her community obligation and especially wanted to help because of her brother. She only did it the one day. She found it fun seeing all of the soldiers but her husband was right. They did whistle!

Arthur Wolf helped his mother, who headed the women's group of the American Lutheran Church in Eustis, Nebraska. Summer sausage was a special treat for the soldiers. Twelve dozen eggs were carefully packed and taken to the Canteen for use in the many angel food cakes baked for the soldiers' birthdays.

Arthur had two brothers who served in the military. One in the Navy and one in the Army. He grew up and married a girl named **Gladys** from Farnam, Nebraska. She worked there with her mom as well when it was her community's turn. Sugar was rationed but every town was quite clever with substitutions. Farnam was no different. They used molasses in their popcorn balls.

After her high school graduation, Gladys took a troop train to California to find work. She bravely made the trip all alone from Nebraska to California. The trip went well until the end when she'd taken her shoes off, stumbled, and broke her toe!

A photo of Henry while
he was in the service.

Henry S. Haynes (Hank) went through the North Platte Canteen in December of 1944. Hank was part of a unit training as replacements for those who fell in the front lines. He was sent to the Pacific with four other soldiers. Within nine months, coincidentally about the same time it takes to bring a new life into the world, two of those were killed and the other three were wounded.

Hank was wounded on Mother's Day, 1945. He was on his belly. His buddy wasn't so lucky, he was on his knees. A grenade ended his life that day. Hank spent 108 days in hospitals and had his 25th birthday during his recovery.

A photo of Helen at the time
the Canteen was in operation.

Rae Wilson became ill from the stress and responsibility of leading so many volunteers full time, after March 1942, she relocated for health reasons to Los Angeles, California. **Helen Christ** stepped forward and led the canteen as her replacement. Helen's husband was a Union Pacific train conductor.

Mr. and Mrs.
John Spelts

June and her sister

As time went by, the people interviewed in this book aged. Today they are in their 80's and 90's. They all share two things in common—very patriotic and giving attitudes.

Elberta Brummert is retired from the library. She has her own library of inspirational photo albums.

Lloyd Synovec will still make any piano "talk" if you give him the chance!

John Spelts worked for the railroad as a fireman/oiler for twenty-eight years. He died while the book was in the process of publish.

Ann Perlinger still has the card the serviceman sent her from the popcorn ball when she was only nine years old.

Gene Slattery has a prized trophy that was sent to him. It portrays him wearing short pants. Farm boys never wore such clothes at that time. It is a beautiful and meaningful keepsake, though, for his "above average" kid efforts.

June Kerkman resides in Elgin, Nebraska. She attended Endorf's third talk on the North Platte Canteen, April 18, 2012 at the Elgin Senior Center.

Pearl Nickerson resides in Lexington, Nebraska. She attended Endorf's first talk on the North Platte Canteen, April 15, 2012 at the Lexington Public Library.

Lorene and Doris

John Zgud has the map he carried in his pocket in case he would get lost.

Meadowlark Pointe in Cozad, Nebraska was a hot spot for locating those who had lived the subject. Endorf, dressed in Navy WAVE attire to represent resident **Betty Matz**, spoke on May 30, 2012 in return for the ten stories received at this location from residents and visitors. **Paul Kjar** and **Arthur Wolf** passed away while this book was being prepared for publication.

Doris Kugler and Lorene Huebner just retired from extensive travel, doing professional speaking.

Maurice Stalnaker resides in Norfolk, Nebraska. He attended Endorf's fourth talk on the North Platte Canteen, May 8, 2012 at the Park Avenue Christian School.

Henry Haynes resides in Auburn, Nebraska. Endorf has given the Canteen talk over a dozen times. He was in her crowd on June 3, 2012 at the Brock Christian Church, wearing his purple heart coat with pride during the interview. He is now 92 years young and has been married 59 years.

Tastefully Done

Look lively, my boys! All aboard is the shout!
Wave a goodbye! This trains' pulling out.
Young ladies all smile and blow them a kiss,
These recruits give a yell, they know they'll be missed.
It's time to clean up at the North Platte Canteen.
On the broom and the mop are Sue and Eileen.
There are lots of plates and spoons to be scrubbed.
The ladies will work out of kindness and love.
New bread must be baked and sandwiches made.
Darlene and Betty have brought in three cakes.
Fred just backed in with fresh apples and pears.
Someone dropped off six tables and nine chairs.
The schedule is posted when the boys will be here.
The town will be ready with friendship and cheer.
These lads will be telling a place they call home.
The canteen gives a moment of comfort and hope.
World War II carries on and ladies were there,
The canteen open to show that they cared.
The old depot planks clatter, a train has stopped by,
Welcome! Come in! We have cookies and pie!
Good bye and God bless! As they went on their way!
The schedule reports of more busy days.
They carried the fight to the hard bitter end,
Remembering Nebraska as a patriotic friend.
The old men returned to capture the scene,
Looking for someone to hug at the North Platte Canteen.

Nivan Hornik, published poet, *Rhyming Reflections*

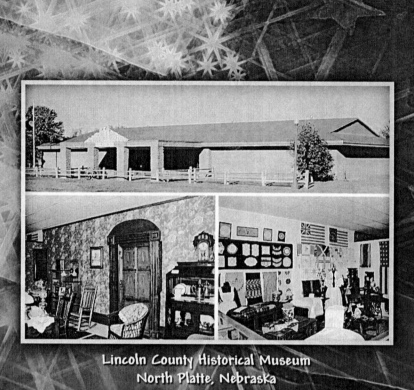

Lincoln County Historical Museum
North Platte, Nebraska

We thank the museum for allowing
us to use their many photographs.

Additional Information
and a Brief "To Do" List

Study this history now. 1,000 World War II Veterans are passing away daily. They are nearly 90 and even older. Sit down and chat with one today.

Visit the 100th Meridian Museum in Cozad, Nebraska to see the actual uniform of Betty Matz. (206 E. 8th)

Visit the Lincoln County Historical Museum in North Platte, Nebraska to see the home of the famous World War II Canteen. (2303 North Buffalo Bill Ave.)

For 51 months every day until the last train went through at about 11 p.m., men and women of every troop train were greeted with the simple gesture of warmth and caring hospitality.

Rae Wilson returned from California for a visit in September 1945 and was present with Helen Christ for the official canteen closing on April 1, 1946.

On August 14, 1946, North Platte hosted a Canteen Reunion celebration in which volunteers from all involved surrounding communities were honored. About twenty thousand turned out in tribute to a gift given to six million.

Rae married Frank H. Sleight, who spent most of his four years of war service in the European Theater of Operations. They lived in North Platte. In 1955 they moved to Lincoln. She returned to live in North Platte after 1982.

Helen Christ died of cancer in 1956 after being ill for four years.

Hirschfeld's still exists. It is now operated by Joe's grandson. Stop to shop and share stories at: 401 N. Dewey (Downtown) North Platte, Nebraska.

Other recommended writing and film documentary about this subject: *Once Upon A Town* by Bob Greene, *North Platte Canteen* by James Reisdorff and *The Canteen Spirit* (DVD) by PBS (all on Amazon).

We are all travelers in the wilderness of this world, and the best we can find in our travels is an honest friend.

-Robert Louis Stevenson

Sarah and Cory Doty

Katie Robinson

Shari Apking

Lela Newcombe

Dedication and Acknowledgments

This book is dedicated to Charlotte's daughter
and son-in-law, Sarah and Cory.

Love is patient and kind.
Love is not jealous or boastful or proud.

1 Corinthians 13:4

A giant thanks to my photographer, Katie Robinson, for taking time out of her busy schedule to work with me, sometimes juggling three things at once to meet my deadlines. What an incredible friend and mentor. Words cannot express how much I value our long lasting friendship.

I appreciate each family member for taking time out of busy schedules to drop everything and work with me. Most met me for the first time as the Lord led me on this new journey. It was a great pleasure to learn the individual experiences and build the trust it takes to work with the stories I write, not an easy feat to make my self-imposed deadline. Thanks again for your cooperation. I believe this is a wonderful piece of historic work that many will cherish for years to come.

The careful editing eyes of Shari Apking and Lela Newcombe are treasured beyond measure. I could always count on them when I was stumped for proper wording.

Charlotte Endorf

About The Author

Charlotte Endorf is a lifelong Nebraskan, a dual member of Toastmasters International who twice earned the Distinguished Toastmaster award. She is designated as one of the five high use speakers with the Nebraska Humanities Council. Her Humanities topics are: The Orphan Train, The Life and Legacy of Annie Oakley, Notable Nebraskan – Tillie Olsen and The North Platte Canteen. She speaks to schools, colleges, women's groups, museums, town festivals, senior centers, and libraries throughout Nebraska. Endorf and her daughter, Sarah, have authored several books together: *After the Rain, Oh the Beautiful Rainbow, Plains Bound: Fragile Cargo, and By Train They Came: Volume 1 and 2.* Endorf also developed a documentary on the Orphan Train riders for the Madison County Historical Society, a CD after a trip to New York City, *Unsung Neighbors, They Call Me Teddy, Trains of Promise,* and *My Wooden Spoon.*

She was nominated by the Madison County Historical Society and selected by American Mothers, Inc. as Nebraska's 2011 Mother of the Year. She resides in Hadar with her husband, son, and two dogs. She is an avid reader and enjoys listening to books while she journeys every direction, thousands of miles each year to share her stories across the state and meet many new friends. Her family started the second Free Little Library in Nebraska for their community in their own front yard.

Ethan Nelson

About The Illustrator

Ethan Nelson lives on a family farm and ranch in the Nebraska Panhandle with his dad, mom and older brother Jake. The scenery of western Nebraska provides Ethan with ever-changing vistas of sky and clouds and animals and the challenge of capturing them on canvas or on camera.

Ethan began his career of drawing and painting at a young age. One of his earliest artistic accomplishments was the 2002 Nebraska Fence Post Christmas Art Contest where, at the age of five, he received his first award. In 2007 Ethan joined the Cheyenne County Art Guild. That same year Ethan and his older brother Jake launched their business, Nelsonart©, which specializes in original art notecards.

Ethan's artwork has received recognition at the local, state and national levels. Nelsonart© has earned entrepreneurship awards and has been featured in the Nebraska Fence Post, The High Plains Journal, Nebraska Aviation PIREPS, The Sidney Sun-Telegraph, and the Scottsbluff Star Herald.

The young artist has improved his marketing and art skills with on line website construction classes, graphics and photography classes through the Western Nebraska Community College. He is currently a high school sophomore at the Nelson Home School.

Ethan would like to express his appreciation for the Cheyenne County Art Guild for critiques and support in his art endeavors, artist Judy McElroy for her instruction with watercolors, and artist Rachelle Eversole for instruction and help with oils.

Nelsonart© can be found at www.nelsonart.webs.com, www.cheyennecountyartguildblogspot.com, and on Facebook.

"You have not lived until you have done something for someone who can never repay you."
– Author Unknown

Index

Kugler, Doris - 31

Lydiatt, Maurine - 33

Matz, Betty - 25

Nickerson, Pearl - 21

Perlinger, Ann - 15

Runner, Robert - 13

Schroeder, Martha - 45

Slattery, Gene - 17

Spelts, John - 11

Stalaker, Maurice - 41

Stuart, Margaret - 43

Synovec, Lloyd - 8

Tastefully Done - 57

Today – 53

Wilson, Rae - 3

Wolf, Arthur & Gladys - 47

Zgud, John - 23

Titles by author Charlotte Endorf!

After the Rain, Oh the Beautiful Rainbow!
A-Z of Overcoming All Types of Obstacles
A collaboration with her daughter, Sarah Mae Endorf. $12.95

Learn more about the Orphan Train with these items.

Plains Bound: Fragile Cargo; Revealing Orphan Train Reality $14.95

Ordinary Orphan Train Riders Who Became
   Extraordinary Friends - DVD Documentary $15.00

By Train They Came; Fragile Excess Baggage - Volume 1 $24.95

By Train They Came;
   Fragile Excess Baggage - Volume 2 $27.95

Trains of Promise - A Collection of Stories and Recipes $18.95

They Call Me Teddy!
   In memory of the Orphan Train riders who were given dogs $13.95
   when they found their new homes.

Poetry of an Orphan Train rider and Nebraska author. $15.00

Follow the marvelous journey of an author. $19.95

Charlotte's journey as Nebraska Mother of the Year. $15.95

The heartwarming story of the North Platte Canteen. $15.95

Name: _____   Subtotal $_____
Address: _____   Sales Tax (NE 5.5%) $_____
City/State/Zip: _____   Shipping $6.00
Phone: _____   Total $_____

Endorf Enterprises · 402 Sycamore, Hadar, NE 68701
402-371-3701 · endorf@cableone.net · www.unsungneighbors.com

CPSIA information can be obtained
at www.ICGtesting.com
Printed in the USA
FFOW04n1632150415
12647FF

National Parks
Olympic

AUDRA WALLACE

Children's Press®
An Imprint of Scholastic Inc.

Content Consultant

James Gramann, PhD

Professor, Department of Recreation, Park and Tourism Sciences

Texas A&M University, College Station, Texas

Library of Congress Cataloging-in-Publication Data
Names: Wallace, Audra.
Title: Olympic / by Audra Wallace.
Description: New York, NY : Children's Press, an imprint of Scholastic Inc., 2018. | Series: A true
    book | Includes bibliographical references and index.
Identifiers: LCCN 2017025791 | ISBN 9780531235089 (library binding) | ISBN 9780531238110 (pbk.)
Subjects: LCSH: Olympic National Park (Wash.)—Juvenile literature.
Classification: LCC F897.O5 W349 2018 | DDC 979.7/98—dc23
LC record available at https://lccn.loc.gov/2017025791

Scholastic Inc., 557 Broadway, New York, NY 10012

1 2 3 4 5 6 7 8 9 10 R 27 26 25 24 23 22 21 20 19 18

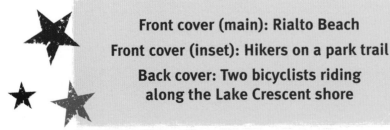

Front cover (main): Rialto Beach

Front cover (inset): Hikers on a park trail

**Back cover: Two bicyclists riding
along the Lake Crescent shore**

Find the Truth!

Everything you are about to read is true *except* for one of the sentences on this page.

Which one is **TRUE**?

T or F   Olympic National Park's glaciers have been growing in recent years.

T or F   Some trees in the park are more than 200 feet (61 meters) tall.

Find the answers in this book.

Contents

THE BIG TRUTH!

National Parks Field Guide: Olympic

Olympic chipmunk

4

A field of wildflowers

Bald eagle

Olympic National Park is home to more than 73 miles (117 kilometers) of coastline.

CHAPTER 1

A Long History

The Olympic **Peninsula** in Washington State is often called "a gift from the sea"—and for good reason! From ice-capped mountains and dense rain forests to rushing rivers and rugged shores, there is a lot to explore. This diverse and beautiful area is home to Olympic National Park, one of the most popular parks in the U.S. National Park System. More than three million people visit the park each year.

Olympic National Park

Born Beneath the Waves

The Olympic Peninsula was formed millions of years ago as lava spewed from volcanoes on the Pacific Ocean floor. Over time, the hardened lava built up to form underwater mountains. Then, about 35 million years ago, two of the huge plates that make up Earth's crust crashed into each other. One of the plates pushed the underwater mountains up above the waves. Today, these mountains are known as the Olympic Mountains.

The Olympic Mountains formed when one piece of Earth's crust moved under another, forcing it upward.

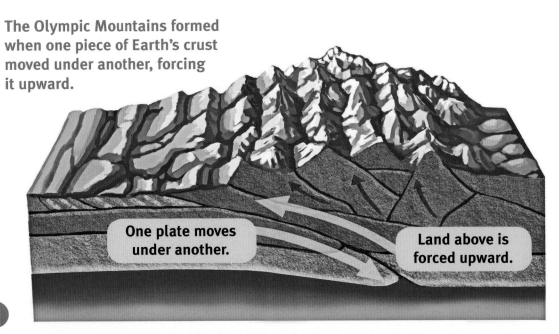

One plate moves under another.

Land above is forced upward.

You can still see ancient Makah carvings of whales and people at Wedding Rocks along the coast of the park.

A Land of Many People

People first set foot on the peninsula more than 10,000 years ago. Eight Native American groups eventually settled there. They are the Hoh, Lower Elwha Klallam, Jamestown S'Klallam, Port Gamble S'Klallam, Quileute, Quinault, Skokomish, and Makah. These early peoples hunted the area's many deer and elk. Shellfish, salmon, and marine mammals such as seals and whales were also important sources of food.

Early Explorers

An explorer named Juan de Fuca is believed to be the first European to explore the Olympic Peninsula. In 1592, he claimed the body of water along the peninsula's northern coast for Spain. As a result, this narrow strip of water was named after him. Explorers from other countries, including France and England, soon followed in de Fuca's footsteps.

A Timeline of Olympic National Park

1850s

Native American groups give up their claim to Olympic Peninsula land in a series of treaties.

1788

British explorer Captain John Meares names the park's tallest peak, Mount Olympus, after the mythical home of ancient Greek gods.

1885

Lieutenant Joseph O'Neil leads the first major expedition into the Olympic Mountains.

A Struggle to Survive

The arrival of Europeans had a devastating effect on Olympic's Native American population. Diseases such as smallpox and influenza killed thousands of people. Native Americans also competed with the new settlers for food and land. In the 1850s, the U.S. government forced Olympic's Native Americans onto reservations, or areas of land that was set aside for them, along the shore.

1938

President Franklin D. Roosevelt signs a law creating Olympic National Park.

1958

The number of annual visitors to Olympic National Park reaches one million for the first time.

1977

A farmer discovers the remains of a mastodon, an elephant-like mammal from the Ice Age, just outside of the park.

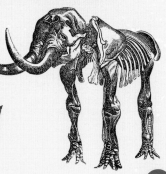

Saving Olympic

By the late 1800s, Olympic's forests had become a hot spot for logging companies and hunters. Trees were cut down for lumber, and elk herds were nearly wiped out. **Conservation** groups

President Theodore Roosevelt

encouraged the U.S. government to protect the area. In 1897, President Grover Cleveland set up the Olympic Forest Reserve. This officially protected the plants and animals living there. Twelve years later, President Theodore Roosevelt made Mount Olympus a national monument. Finally, in 1938, President Franklin D. Roosevelt signed a law creating Olympic National Park.

National Park Fact File

A national park is land that is protected by the federal government. It is a place of importance to the United States because of its beauty, history, or value to scientists. The U.S. Congress creates a national park by passing a law. Here are some key facts about Olympic National Park.

Olympic National Park	
Location	Washington State
Year established	1938
Size	922,651 acres (373,384 hectares)
Average number of visitors each year	More than 3 million
Tallest mountain	Mount Olympus at 7,980 feet (2,432 m)
Deepest lake	Lake Crescent at 624 feet (190 m)

Hikers who reach Olympic's mountaintops are rewarded with an incredible view.

CHAPTER 2

Mighty Mountains and More

Giant jagged mountains rise into the clouds above Olympic. The tallest of them is Mount Olympus, at a height of 7,980 feet (2,432 m). Glaciers cover some of the mountains. These thick sheets of ice formed millions of years ago during the Ice Age. Today, there are 60 named glaciers in the park. The most famous is Blue Glacier, which is more than 2.6 miles (4.2 km) long.

The amount of ice that makes up Blue Glacier is equal to about 20 trillion ice cubes.

Visitors who plan to travel along Hurricane Ridge should check the weather and wind speeds before going.

Hair-Raising Hikes

Harsh weather and icy ground make it very dangerous and difficult to climb Olympic's highest mountains. Most of the park's visitors walk or ski along the trail to Hurricane Ridge instead. This spot offers breathtaking views of the park's mountains. But if you want to check out this area, beware: It is named Hurricane Ridge for the powerful winds that blow across it. They can reach speeds of up to 75 miles per hour (121 kilometers per hour)!

Rock Stars

In some spots along Olympic's shores, tall towers of rock stick up from the sand. These formations are called sea stacks. Some are more than 40 feet (12 m) tall. Over time, wind and waves have carved the sea stacks into a variety of fascinating shapes. Some sea stacks even have trees growing on top of them!

A wooden bridge is located above Sol Duc Falls, providing visitors with a stunning view of the water.

Go With the Flow

More than 4,000 miles (6,437 km) of rivers and streams make their way down the sides of the Olympic Mountains. Some of these waterways spill over rocky cliffs as waterfalls. The park's most popular waterfall is Sol Duc Falls. It flows into hot springs, which are pools of water that are heated by underground **magma**. The hot springs are like big, warm baths. Park visitors soak in them to relax.

Lots of Lakes

If you enjoy fishing, you'll find plenty of opportunities to cast a line at Olympic. The park is home to 600 lakes, and they are filled with a wide variety of fish. Lake Crescent is the park's deepest lake, at 624 feet (190 m). Its clear blue water is packed with Beardslee and Crescenti cutthroat trout. These freshwater fish are only found in Olympic. They feed on kokanee, a type of sockeye salmon.

Visitors can take boats or kayaks out on Lake Crescent to catch fish.

CHAPTER 3

Wildlife on the Move

Many different animals roam through Olympic National Park, especially in its forests and meadows. Herds of Roosevelt elk graze on ferns, shrubs, and **lichens**. Black-tailed deer can be spotted nibbling on grass. Mountain lions prowl these areas, too. They hide behind shrubs and small trees, hoping to catch an elk or a deer for dinner.

 Roosevelt elk are named after Theodore Roosevelt, the 26th U.S. president.

Into the Woods

Spotted owls also call the park's forests home. They peek out from the trees as Douglas squirrels scamper across the ground below. Millions of banana slugs creep along the forest floor. These slimy 6-inch (15-centimeter) creatures gobble up dead leaves and decaying plants. Other forest dwellers include black bears, snowshoe hares, Pacific tree frogs, and rough-skinned newts.

Barred owls such as this one first arrived in Olympic National Park and the surrounding region as recently as the 20th century.

A humpback whale breaches, or jumps from the water.

Ocean Life

Down by the sea, bald eagles soar overhead. They nest in trees along the beaches. Sea otters float on thick beds of kelp, a type of seaweed. Pacific harbor seals snuggle up on small islands, while orcas dive in and out of the waves. Many people go whale-watching on boats in hopes of seeing a humpback or gray whale on the move.

Migrating coho salmon swim against the current.

A River Adventure

During the summer and early fall, coho salmon **migrate** more than 50 miles (80 km) from the Pacific Ocean to the park's Sol Duc River. There the fish spawn, or lay eggs. Along their journey, they can be seen leaping over a set of small waterfalls called the Salmon Cascades. Bull trout, steelhead, and four other salmon species also travel through the park's rivers and streams. Amphibians such as Cope's salamanders and tailed frogs live there, too.

Special Species

A few animals found in Olympic National Park are not found anywhere else in the world. They include the Olympic marmot, a large rodent that burrows underground and is very social with its fellow marmots. Insects such as the Quileute gazelle beetle and Hulbirt's skipper (a type of butterfly) are also found here. Olympic even has its own unique grasshopper species!

An Olympic marmot keeps watch outside its den.

National Parks Field Guide:
Olympic

Field guides have helped people identify wildlife and natural objects from birds to rocks for more than 100 years. Guides usually contain details about appearance, common locations, and other basics. Use this field guide to discover six animals you can spot in the park, and learn fascinating facts about each one!

Roosevelt elk

Scientific name: *Cervus elaphus roosevelti*

Habitat: From mountain meadows and forests to lowland rain forests

Diet: Ferns, shrubs, and lichens from the rain forest; meadow grasses

Fact: A male elk can weigh up to 1,100 pounds (500 kilograms).

Olympic marmot

Scientific name: *Marmota olympus*

Habitat: Mountain meadows above 4,000 feet (1,219 m)

Diet: Flowering plants such as lupine and glacier lilies; plant roots

Fact: This housecat-sized mammal lets out a loud whistle to warn other marmots of predators in the area.

Orca

Scientific name: *Orcinus orca*

Habitat: Ocean; often spotted along the west coast of the United States and Canada

Diet: Fish, squid, birds, other marine animals

Fact: This "killer whale" hunts in pods, or groups, of 5 to 30 whales.

Rhinoceros auklet

Scientific name: *Cerorhinca monocerata*

Habitat: Along the coasts and open sea of the northern Pacific Ocean

Diet: Mainly fish

Fact: This seabird is named for the "horn" on the base of its bill.

Sea otter

Scientific name: *Enhydra lutris*

Habitat: Shallow waters along the northern Pacific coast

Diet: Fish, crabs, sea urchins, clams, abalones, mussels, snails

Fact: This marine mammal uses rocks to crack open the shells of the shellfish it eats.

Olympic chipmunk

Scientific name: *Tamias amoenus caurinus*

Habitat: Forests and meadows

Diet: Seeds, nuts, berries, insects

Fact: This small mammal has large cheek pouches where it can store food to be eaten later.

Roaming the Rain Forests

You might be surprised to learn that there are rain forests in Olympic National Park. A rain forest is a forest that gets heavy amounts of rain each year. There are two types of rain forests. Tropical rain forests are found near the **equator**, where it is hot. Temperate rain forests, like those in Olympic, are found in cooler regions.

 More than 100 inches (254 cm) of rain falls in Olympic's rain forests each year.

Layers of the Temperate Rain Forest

In the western area of the park lies the Hoh Rain Forest. There, some of the trees are more than 200 feet (61 m) tall. They include western hemlock and Douglas fir. Sitka spruces also grow here. The trunks of these trees can measure up to 60 feet (18 m) around. In the shadier areas beneath these towering treetops are vine maple, sword fern, and vanilla leaf. Far below is the forest floor. The dense collection of vines, ferns, and leaves above keeps most of the sunlight from reaching the floor. It is dark and damp, and mosses and fungi, such as mushrooms, grow here.

The Hoh Rain Forest was once part of a huge rain forest region that stretched from Alaska to California.

Canopy

This is the top layer of treetops, which receives the most sunlight.

Western hemlock

Sitka spruce

Understory

Shade-loving plants flourish here, where the treetops of the canopy block some of the sun.

Vine maple

Sword fern

Forest Floor

Mosses and fungi flourish in the dark dampness of the rain forest's bottom layer.

Zeller's Bolete mushroom

Liverwort

Plenty of Plants

In all, more than 1,100 plant species grow in Olympic National Park. In **alpine** regions, wildflowers such as pink Douglasia and red willow-herb peek out from rocky ledges. They survive strong mountain winds by growing low to the ground. Avalanche lilies, violets, and starflowers can be found farther down the mountains. Common shrubs in the park include blueberry, juniper, and rhododendron.

White avalanche lilies bloom in the mountains of Olympic National Park.

Tree of Life

Native Americans once depended on forests for everything from food and medicine to shelter and transportation. They called the western red cedar the "tree of life." Native people built longhouses and canoes from this tree's rot-resistant wood. Some even carved giant totem poles out of red cedar. These painted sculptures often honored a family's ancestors or symbolized an ancient legend.

This western red cedar, located in the park, is the world's largest of its kind.

33

Workers record the park's sounds. This helps them track how much human noise occurs in the area.

34

The Future of the Park

The National Park Service (NPS) is responsible for conserving Olympic's wild landscape. But one of the biggest threats to the park is out of the NPS's control. Over the past 40 years, Earth's temperature has been rising at a faster pace than usual. Most scientists think that the use of fuels such as coal and oil is to blame. When these fuels are burned, they release gases that trap heat in Earth's **atmosphere**. This has led to a warming of the planet's climate.

A Warming World

Rising temperatures affect Olympic in a big way. Much of the **precipitation** that once fell as snow is now falling as rain. Glaciers need snow to maintain their size. But some have begun to shrink. Others have disappeared completely. During the park's dry summer months, its rivers depend on glaciers for fresh water. Without them, the rivers could run dry and the animals that rely on them—or live in them—will be at risk of dying out.

The glaciers on Mount Olympus and elsewhere are smaller than they were decades ago.

An ancient tree clings to the soil around slowly eroding earth at Kalaloch Creek.

On Shaky Ground

Erosion is another constant challenge for Olympic National Park. Strong winds and waves wear down the park's mountains and rocky coastlines. Park rangers must keep an eye out for loose rocks and tilting trees, especially after a heavy rainfall. Dangerous rockfalls and landslides are common in and around the park.

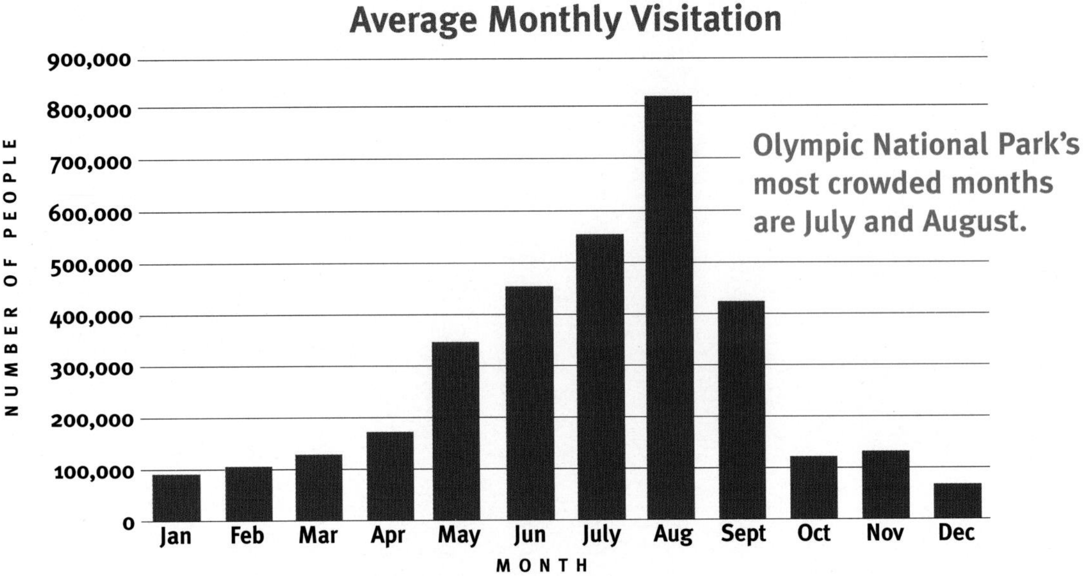
Average Monthly Visitation
NUMBER OF PEOPLE
900,000
800,000
700,000
600,000
500,000
400,000
300,000
200,000
100,000
0
Jan
Feb
Mar
Apr
May
Jun
July
Aug
Sept
Oct
Nov
Dec
MONTH
Olympic National Park's most crowded months are July and August.

Many Kinds of Visitors

Olympic's native plants and animals have a lot of visitors to contend with, from destructive plants to crowds of humans. Each year, the NPS spends millions of dollars to control **invasive species** in Olympic. Plants such as Scot's broom and Japanese knotweed compete with native plants for sunlight and water. Park rangers must pull, cut, or spray these weeds with chemicals to prevent them from taking over. Rangers also work to keep invasive animals such as wood-boring beetles and zebra mussels out of the park.

The number of people visiting Olympic is on the rise. This makes keeping it clean a tough task. During the summer, people flock to the park to camp, fish, and hike. But they also leave behind a lot of trash. The park provides recycling bins and encourages people to reduce the amount of waste they bring on their trip. By helping to keep the park clean, visitors can play an important role in preserving its natural beauty for years to come. ★

If people are careful and responsible, Olympic National Park will remain a beautiful sight for many years to come.

Map Mystery

About 300 years ago, a mudslide buried a Makah village. A hiker discovered this buried settlement in 1970. More than 55,000 objects from the past were found there. Along what body of water was the village located? Follow the directions below to find the answer.

Directions

1. Start at the park's tallest peak.

2. Hike northwest to the pools of water heated by magma.

3. Travel south to a nearby rain forest.

4. You're almost there! Head west to the beach named after red gemstones.

5. Go north along the coast, then look east to see the banks of this lake.

Strait of Juan de Fuca

Wedding Rocks

Lake Ozette

US 101

Sol Duc Riv

PACIFIC OCEAN

Ruby Beach

Area of map
U.S.

Alaska and Hawai'i are not drawn to scale or placed in their proper places.

OLYMPIC NATIONAL PARK

Olympic National Park Visitor Center

Park Headquarters

Lake Crescent

Storm King Ranger Station

Sol Duc Hot Springs

Sol Duc Falls

Hurricane Ridge

Hurricane Ridge Visitor Center

Hoh Rain Forest

□ *Blue Glacier*

△ *Mount Olympus*

Hoh Rain Forest Visitor Center

Quinault Rain Forest Ranger Station

Staircase Ranger Station

USFS/NPS Recreation Information

Compass Rose
North
West — East
South

Be an ★ Animal Tracker!

If you're ever in Olympic National Park, keep an eye out for these animal tracks. They'll help you know which animals are in the area.

Bald eagle
Foot length: 6 inches (15 cm)

Beaver
Hind foot length: 6 to 7 inches (15 to 18 cm)

Black-tailed deer
Hoof length: 3.5 inches (9 cm)

Mountain lion
Paw length: 2 to 4 inches (5 to 10 cm)

Olympic black bear
Front paw length: 2 to 5 inches
(5 to 12.5 cm)

Snowshoe hare
Paw length: 4 to 5.5 inches
(10 to 14 cm)

True Statistics

Number of years since Olympic Peninsula formed: About 35 million

Number of visitors in 2016: 3,390,221

Number of archaeological sites: 650

Number of major rivers: 13

Total distance covered by trails in the park: 611 miles (983.3 km)

Number of named glaciers: 60

Biggest glacier: Blue Glacier at almost 2 square miles (5.2 sq km)

Annual rainfall along the coast and western-facing valleys: Up to 170 inches (431.8 cm)

Annual snowfall on Mount Olympus: 50 to 70 feet (15.2 to 21.3 m)

Did you find the truth?

(F) Olympic National Park's glaciers have been growing in recent years.

(T) Some trees in the park are more than 200 feet (61 meters) tall.

Resources

Books

Benoit, Peter. *Temperate Forests*. New York: Children's Press, 2011.

Flynn, Sarah Wassner, and Julie Beer. *National Parks Guide U.S.A.* Washington, DC: National Geographic, 2016.

Stein, R. Conrad. *Washington*. New York: Children's Press, 2015.

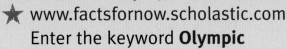

Visit this Scholastic website for more information on Olympic National Park:
★ www.factsfornow.scholastic.com
Enter the keyword **Olympic**

Important Words

alpine (AL-pine) having to do with mountains

atmosphere (AT-muhs-feer) the mixture of gases that surrounds a planet

conservation (kahn-sur-VAY-shuhn) the protection of valuable resources, especially wildlife and plants

equator (ih-KWAY-tur) an imaginary line around the middle of Earth that is an equal distance from the North and South Poles

invasive species (in-VAY-siv SPEE-sheez) an animal or plant that moves into an area and alters or harms the plants or animals that are found there

lichens (LYE-kuhnz) flat, spongelike growth that consists of algae and fungi growing close together

magma (MAG-muh) melted rock found beneath Earth's surface

migrate (MYE-grate) to move to another area or climate at a particular time of year

peninsula (puh-NIN-suh-luh) a piece of land that sticks out from a larger landmass and is almost completely surrounded by water

precipitation (pri-sip-ih-TAY-shuhn) the falling of water from the sky in the form of rain, sleet, hail, or snow

Index

Page numbers in **bold** indicate illustrations.

About the Author

Audra Wallace graduated from Ithaca College, where she studied film production and elementary education. Her passion for writing nonfiction and teaching kids led her to a position with Scholastic. Since 2006, Wallace has written and edited the award-winning classroom magazine *Scholastic News* Edition 3. She and her family enjoy exploring the great outdoors near their home in New York—and beyond!